Frenzy

Understanding The Mind
of A Drug Addict

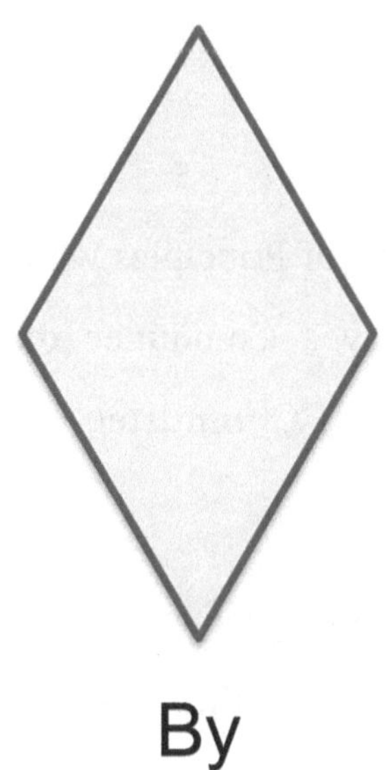

By

Alicia J. Fasshauer

otherwise, by any usage or abuse of any policies, processes, or directions contained within is the sole and utter responsibility of the recipient reader. Under no circumstances will any legal responsibility or blame be held against the publisher for any reparation, damages, or monetary loss due to the information herein, either directly or indirectly.

Respective authors own all copyrights not held by the publishcr.

The information herein is offered for informational purposes solely and is universal as so. The presentation of the information is without a contract or any type of guarantee assurance.

The trademarks that are used are without any consent, and the publication of the trademark is without permission or backing by the trademark owner. All trademarks and brands within this book are for clarifying purposes only and are owned by the owners themselves, not affiliated with this document.

Table of Contents

Introduction:

A young girl once told me that she was afraid of the telephone ringing. In class she would start shaking just because of a call. No one in school knew of her affliction, but it was caused by a fear for her drug addicted mother. Her deepest anxiety was that this time it would be the call. It would be any number of destructive stories of how her mom had overdosed, or got shot looking for drugs on the street. And one day when that call did happen, the fear had been there so long that she didn't even feel afraid. It was just confusion.

Watching someone you love spiral down that fate, is one of the worst things that can happen to anyone. You love them, you want to help them, but sometimes helping them will only keep them trapped longer. The distinction between enabling and helping is very close together, and it is sometimes like walking on a trapeze line. One way too far in either direction will lose them forever. The action of enabling is when you "support a drug addict in such a way that you keep them from experiencing the naturally occurring consequences of their actions." This can show up in such ways as allowing them to live in your house, buying them groceries, and giving them money. They need a low to experience salvation, because only through this rock bottom will they ask for help.

In researching for this book, I interviewed several addicts to give it perspective. I have changed their names for the sake of their privacy, but they all have a very important messages to convey. One of these women is a middle aged heroine user we'll call

Kate. She started using opioids in her late twenties after a car accident. Kate had a loving family that was more than willing to support her, but she spiraled out of control. It got so bad at one point that she couldn't hold down a job. So her father took her in, and offered to take care of her. As anyone who is given kindness, she appreciates and remarks on it. However, she also says, "I wish he had kicked me out on the streets. I always had everything given to me, and it never made me want to change. It took me 20 years to finally realize all the time I lost."

Drug Addiction isn't something that you can just stop because you know it's good for you. Faced with the threat of withdrawal, and an unbearable need for the drug, it seems almost impossible to quit. Kate reflects by saying that withdrawal is "like having the worst flu imaginable and a severe cold at the same time. But the worst part is your mind is also constantly going crazy. You have anxiety, sweating, goosebumps, and diarrhea leaking out your butt. But a non-addict has no idea what the anxiety is like, how intense it is. The anxiety is the worst part." It is a sensation that you and I just can't understand. We can see it, but we can't see the devastation left behind when the drugs are pulled away.

I became involved in this world when my son suffered a sports related injury at the age of 15. When he recovered from the physical injury, we thought that the worst was over. What we didn't know was that an opioid addiction was left behind. He would search out friends and peers looking for stronger prescriptions, and behind our backs he increased his dosage from one or two a day to five or more a day. He became erratic and someone we hardly recognized.

The problem for you and me, is that we expect them just to snap out of it. Why would you do that? We love you, can't you just stop? Flushing pills down the toilet, nagging them to quit, and forcing them into rehabs are not cures. As much as we all would like them to work, it just doesn't. Quitting isn't as simple as being told to quit. Life has to push them in that direction. Only when they are ready to come to you, can you begin to get them treatment.

Facing the confusion of a problem I just couldn't solve, that's when I started looking for my own answers. I found Al-Anon, an organization that supports the family and friends of addicts. There are so many people with similar stories, and best of all I realized I wasn't alone. Though our stories are different, the problem remains the same. The one we love has a problem, and this has created chaos in all our lives. But now I didn't have to face these problems without any guidance or experience, there are others who have seen the same things. Creating acceptance around the idea of addiction as a disease, and understanding that I was unable to prevent their bad choices, was important for my future. Addiction isn't just a sickness for the addict, but one for the whole family.

For Zachary
We Love You

Chapter One:

What It Feels Like to

Be Addicted

As I attempted to tackle the emotional turmoil of addiction, the one thing that distanced me from the addict I loved was information. I just couldn't imagine what it was to need something like that. The concept of withdrawal was foreign to me, and though depicted in movies it seemed unreal. In a way, it put a wall between them and me because I didn't have understanding. I was asking, what can I do to help you? But he needed more than that. He needed to know that I wanted to understand. He needed me to ask, what does it feel like to be you?

A metaphor that made a lot of sense to me, is to compare it to quitting food. Your body physically needs food to live, and your brain is dependent on it. Remove the food, and what happens? You get hungry, cranky, and nauseated. . . and the longer this goes on, the worse these symptoms get. What do you even do without this routine? Everyday, you get up, brush your teeth, and eat breakfast. What happens to that time now? How do you cope in such a way that food isn't always the one thing you're thinking about.

You have to do something, or it won't get out of your head. Even as you try to distract yourself, you think of how it would be so easy to walk to the pantry, cook up some food, and eat it right there. But you don't. One day follows another day, and you follow your routine. Until you don't. Even as you take the first bite you feel ashamed, but you can't stop now. That is true desperation, and that is what addiction is.

But even still, I couldn't understand why he would act like that. Would I steal for food? I don't know. I have never been at that point. The truth is that I have never experienced true desperation. But, I could attempt to understand it. Addiction is like being possessed by a demon. He comes into these people's lives, and takes control of their brains. However, he leaves the consciousness behind. So these people are left with their bodies being manipulated, unable to stop it on their own, watching every action they make. They are aware of their crimes, but all they can think is "how did I get here?" They don't know how to get out. They just know that this is the only thing in their life now.

Is it any wonder that addicts have trouble asking for help. They spend so much time high, that when the moment of clarity finally comes over them, who do they call? The grandmother they stole from? The girlfriend they betrayed? The friend they get high with? . . . Who is left in their life that is willing to talk to them about addiction?

So when your loved one calls you at three in the morning, pick up the phone. It might be them just asking for money, but it also might be the phone conversation that saves their life.

Chapter Two:

The Brain is Changed by Addiction

Addiction is a disease. It is a simple statement, but one that is often disputed. There is a stigma in addiction unlike any other psychological disease, and it begins with centuries of misunderstanding. It was believed that these people are weak willed, immoral, or just looking to have a good time. But addicts don't want to use drugs. They have to use them. They are DRIVEN to use them. They have no control over this "frenzy" what so ever.

The prefrontal cortex is the part of the brain that makes decisions, and addicts lose just that. Their ability to make their own decisions. When the prefrontal cortex is overrun by the addiction, they lose their capability to follow social and biological norms. Overtime, the scientific opinion of addiction has grown and changed. It is not without its flaws, but it is developing into something that can actually help.

The first time we began to truly understand addiction was through the rat experiment of the 1950s. It wasn't an attempt to study addiction at all, but as every great thing, an accident. James Old and David Milner decided to apply an electric stimulus directly to the brain of a rat. What they didn't know was that they were hitting the pleasure center of the brain, or the nucleus accumbent. Whenever they shocked these rats, they received extreme gratification. Milner and Old noticed this addictive response, and they began upping their experiments.

They set up a maze with a strong electric grid in between the rat and the desired stimulation. However, this wasn't just any grid. It was so painful that a starving rat wouldn't cross it to get to food. When an addicted rat was given the same option, an electric grid didn't stop it.

The longer we study addiction, the more we find that addiction is extremely complicated and sadly completely misunderstood. When various studies try to simplify the cause of addiction, it often results in misunderstanding and confusion. It is not one thing, but the result of your environment, genetics, and stress. Misguidance in such statements as "it is only a chemical reaction" or "it is only their environment," is just untrue. Psychology is complicated, and not defined by simplicities.

Keep this in mind as I mentioned another monumental study, and this is the rat pack study of the 1970s. It was performed by Dr. Bruce Alexander, and he wondered what would happen if his addicted rats were given a community. Up until this point, addiction was only studied in solitary. When rats were given the choice between regular water and drug laced water, they drank from the drug laced one until they overdosed. However, Alexander made a rat paradise where they had everything they could want. He noticed that when the rats had a community, they still drank from the drug laced water, but they did it in more moderation. The rats did not overdose like they did in solitary. This speaks to how isolation contributes to drug addiction, and how you need others to get through this disease.

However as I mentioned earlier, addiction is caused by various factors, and to understand this better you must learn a little more about the brain. The change of an addict's brain begins with the first time they use it. The pleasure center of the brain is flooded with dopamine, leading you to want to do it again. To put this in perspective, sex floods your brain with about 50 to 100 times the normal amount of dopamine. Meanwhile, hardcore drugs flood it 300 to 800 times. In essence, it makes your Nucleus Accumbent (Pleasure Center) numb over time. This is why an addict needs a stronger and stronger dose, more and more often. Your body stops producing its own dopamine, and eventually you need drugs just to feel normal.

This is also a symptom of the extended amygdala becoming more sensitive. This is the part of the brain in control of motivating factors such as anxiety and unease. When the drug high fades, the anxiety produced by the extended amygdala is what's left behind. As time passes, this part of the brain becomes increasingly sensitive, causing more and more anxiety. This is part of the reason an addict always needs to get more drugs. They go into a "frenzy" where all that matters is their next fix. They can't concentrate on anything else. In fact they may have just used their drug of choice and the "frenzy" or panic can start before they even come down.

But even still, what makes an addict lose control of themselves? The best way to describe this process is to relate it to a more familiar addiction. Cigarettes. If you are a smoker, do you remember the first cigarette you smoked? It may not have been a particularly memorable moment, but your brain certainly remembered something.

While you are taking that first puff, your nucleus accumbent is being flooded with dopamine. Your prefrontal cortex takes note of this, and sends a message over to the hippocampus to remember the stimuli. It takes note of the taste, the red brand on the package, and any other interactions that you may have had with the cigarette. So days later, you may see the red package, and you will subconsciously think of cigarettes. For the first time, you will feel an initial desire.

Now normally the amount of pleasure given for a new stimulus decreases over time. But when addiction takes over, every time you see a familiar stimulus, your nucleus accumbent overtakes the prefrontal cortex. This cortex normally decides whether the risk is worth the reward, but the nucleus accumbent is vetoing the prefrontal cortex before it even has a chance. So now when you see someone smoking on tv, you need to smoke one too. You have no choice because your decision making is being overpowered. How can you stop something that you didn't have a choice for in the first place?

As the understanding of addiction progresses, there seems like there is hope. No longer do you need to feel the cravings. There are drugs such as suboxone that work as blockers that keep you from being able to get high from opiates. One such drug that is coming to the market soon is acetylcholine. It successfully prevented relapse in both mice and rats. Though these drugs are not a solution, they make everyone more hopeful for a cure in the future.

Chapter Three:

Helping An Addicted Loved One

The best thing to do if someone you love is in denial, is to simply be there for them. Ask them how they are doing? But try not to directly ask if they are addicted to a substance. This blunt of a question will most likely scare them away. Instead, listen to them.

Many times, drug abuse stems from some sort of mental illness or abuse or neglect in the persons past which drives them to "escape" the memories of the abusive events or also helps them through abusive events.

One study found that 53% of drug abusers also have a serious psychological disorder. Everyone has problems, and oftentimes drugs become a coping mechanism to escape these problems. So if your loved one is talking to you about how they feel, that is a step in its own. They are opening up, and they are letting themselves feel emotions that the drugs have been blocking out. Below are some of the best steps to helping your friend or family member find sobriety:

Be Patient:

Don't expect them to admit to their addiction after just one meaningful conversation. You must be patient with them. Change isn't something that comes easily, it is something that happens overtime. In many drug rehabilitation facilities, they call this the wheel of change. It is a cycle, not something that happens at the snap of a hand.

It takes a long time for a person to admit to an addiction on their own. Saying it out loud is very scary. It is like facing your deepest fears, and then knowing you have to deal with it. And even once you are done with rehab and are drug free, addiction is still a part of you. Relapses can happen, but it is part of the process. As long as you are there for them when they make mistakes, they will continue to work on themselves.

Don't Tempt Them:

This may seem obvious, but temptations can present themselves in forms you may not expect. Avoid simple things such as telling drug stories and drinking alcohol in front of them. Imagine not being able to eat your favorite food ever again, and your best friend keeps eating it in front of you. This example isn't as extreme as addiction, but it applies.

Be considerate of the ones you love, and you don't let yourself be the stimuli that triggers the need to use.

Spend some time finding options for the one you love. If you don't have much money to afford a private facility, there are many government funded options. These will most likely be free for you. All that you will need to do get treatment is prove the following:

- Official State Residence
- Lack of Income and Insurance
- Legal Residence in US
- Addiction Status / Need for Intervention

Public facilities often don't have the newest interventions, but they can be the difference between life and death. When the one you love tells you of their addiction, have this information already researched. Be prepared to tell them of their options, and be willing to help them through the process. Many times, this isn't a quick solution. It takes time between admitting to their problem and their first day in rehab.

Be prepared to be patient, but with time the help will come.

Don't Support their Addiction:

An addict would do anything to get their next hit, and unfortunately this often means unintentionally hurting the people they love. Whether it is stealing, tricking, or coercing; It all happens. The important thing to remember is that you are not helping them when you are giving them money. Getting help requires a moment of clarity of their own.

Attempt to distance yourself in such a way that there is still open communication, but that the limit is clearly stated. When your family member is in the throws of addiction, the cardinal rule is that you are allowed to be selfish. Think about what you need, not what they need. Whether you are the sibling, child, spouse, parent, or friend; Don't let yourself get caught in keeping them safe. You can't keep them safe. You can't mother them and make everything alright. Everything isn't alright, and putting a bandaid over it won't cure the real problem. The real issue is within them, and only they can change that. So when they ask you for money, housing, food, or any other item.

Say no. Offer a conversation. Offer your love. But
keep saying no until they ask for help.

Be Available to Talk & Listen:

Be there for them when they are ready to talk,
when they open up about addiction. This starts with
not judging them. No one likes to be an addict, and no
one wants to lose everything for their addiction. Let
them talk to you, and make sure to check in on them
consistently. I know you don't want to call up the
person you love, and hear them out of control. But
you love them, and you'll do it. Make sure that they
know you are available for a conversation at any hour
of the day. Drug addicts live different hours, and if that
clarity comes at three in the morning, then saving
their life is worth the waking up. The most important
thing that you can do is remind them that you love
them. That you know they can change and that they
are worth something.

Chapter Four:

Life after Rehab

Will it be different now? That's the million dollar question everyone wants to ask. Will they be that little boy we remember? Will they be loving, thoughtful, and forgiving? How different can it be now?

The answer is yes, it will be different now, but it isn't over. Addiction is a lifelong disease, it doesn't end the moment you walk out of those doors. It doesn't end when you leave a halfway house or when you have been sober 20 years. It is something that an addict will always have in the back of their head. It is something that will be there forever.

When life gets stressful, they are going to think about it. If someone dies, they are going to think, "If only I could have a hit right now?" They know how to get it, and they could get the money. Not doing what they want most each and every day is going to be difficult. Actually, difficult isn't even the correct word, because it is something that none of us can imagine.

It begins with creating a whole new life for yourself. Imagine not being able to do your favorite hobby or spend time with any of your best friends. Instead, an addict now has endless time, and this time needs to be replaced with something. In rehab, an addict is stripped down to the core, and they have to face who they are now. They have to build themselves up in such a way that they will continue saying no to drugs.

The physical withdrawal is the first part of rehab. An addict can not face who they are, until they have healed their body. Many times addicts neglect their body because of substance abuse. So this means they must eat healthy and exercise before they can even begin on who they are. And once they start on their mind, this is when the real progress begins.

Dr. Colin Ross, a famous psychologist on drug therapy, says that the "problem is not the problem." Addicts must begin to understand that this is a coping mechanism, and in order to get better, they need to face what they are coping for. Digging deep into many worries that they have been ignoring for so long through getting high. They have to face each individual wrong, and forgive themselves.

Therapy such as this continues as they start making new connections. They need friends in their lives that are good for them and support them. It is most likely that their old friends were drinking buddies, and going back to them after recovery will bring them back to drugs and alcohol. They need people who are good for them, who care about their sobriety, and want to see them get better.

Even as they leave rehab, a recovering addict needs to learn to keep busy. They need to get back to working, finding hobbies, and attending meetings. They say that recovery is a full time job. In order to get better, an addict must spend as much time working on sobriety as they did getting high. So what is that hobby that will keep them distracted, even as the thought of taking a hit prods at them? It has to be something special. Exercise, art, music, and writing are all great options. They must find this salvation in themselves, and come out a better person.

Recovery is hard. There is no way around it. Making a new person out of someone you thought you knew, is one of the greatest accomplishments possible. Imagine letting go of everything important to you, and having to remind yourself that this is for the best. Doing the good thing isn't always easy, but it is even harder when the devil is always knocking at your door.

Find faith that they will continue to strive to be a better person. Even if they relapse, that's ok. It is part of the process, and as long as they keep going back to recovery they have strength. They have great self control everyday they don't use drugs. Pride them on their work, and let them know you love them. Let them know that they are worth something, and that they can make it. Only time will tell what they will accomplish.

Conclusion

As I come to the end of this book, I want to remind you that success is possible. It may seem helpless now, but give them time. You never know how a person may change. Look at Stephen King, who used for most of his life, and has now recovered. There was a time when he couldn't even remember writing his own books because of his drug use. Look at Robert Downey Jr, who was an addict for most of the nineties. He found recovery in 2002 and revived his career with Iron Man in 2008. Lastly, look at Drew Barrymore. She went into rehab at the age of 13, and continued to have a great acting career afterwards. There is success to be found when you put in the work.

But what about all the normal people who can't afford expensive private rehab? There are so many stories, starting with Kate. I asked her what made her search for help for the first time, and she told me that it was because of her three year old daughter. They had been having a conversation when her daughter had said, "Mommy, you told me I was a gift from god."

"You are honey," Kate said.

Her daughter looked up at Kate and said, "Can I go back?"

At this moment, Kate knew she had to be a better mother. She needed to find help so that she could make life easier for both her daughters. Finding help and changing who you are isn't easy, but it is something she had to do.

Her addiction didn't end just like that. Twenty years later she was still having relapses, but she was trying everyday. She is currently on a methadone program that is working fairly well for her, and she speaks to the struggles in her life. She wishes she could take away all the hurt she caused. But she can't. She has accepted it and is trying to make a difference in the future.

She says that after being in and out of rehab six or seven times, she wanted to give up on herself. To just call herself a lost case and continue. But she speaks to her success. She says she may not have won the war, but she has won this battle. And everyday that she doesn't use drugs, that is another battle won. Never give up and never forget what life could be. She says that for everyone out there who wants to give up on your loved one, don't. Recovery is possible. It might not be tomorrow, ten years from now, or twenty years from now; But there is hope.

Accept them for who they are, someone with a terrible disease. Someone who struggles, fights, and asks for forgiveness everyday. Living as an active addict is a living Hell, everyday, torment. It doesn't end when they enter recovery, but miracles can happen.

One such miracle was Ray. He woke up one day in the yard he had been living on, and realized he didn't know what happened to the time. He had been an addict for 25 years, and of course the court had sent him to rehab before. Those times he didn't get it. But this time, a very chilling realization came over him, he could either commit suicide or attend rehab. He chose rehab. He went to school, got a job, and started living a real life.

Another miracle is Lucy. One day after a black out episode, she realized that she cheated on her boyfriend. She was a person that always had high moral ground, despite her alcohol problem. When she woke up next to a man she didn't know that morning, she knew for the first time that her drinking was hurting the people she loved most. She checked herself into rehab, and started working on herself. She found a love of exercise and hiking, and discovered that her life is much more calm without the alcohol.

Lastly, Angela is a miracle. She started experimenting with heroin and meth at the age of 15. One day she took a hit, and she stopped breathing. When her grandmother found her she was blue and unconscious. It took constant CPR applied by her grandmother to keep her alive until the ambulance arrived. Later she was stable, but the doctors said she would most likely be a vegetable when she awoke. There was no improvement for six months, and then suddenly she started improving. She started going to meetings and making a life for herself. She had a life to live now because of her sobriety. She got lucky. She decided she has to stay sober this time, because who knows what will happen next time?

Miracles happen all the time. There are many successful people that were once addicts, and there are many people who have died from the disease. When you look to the one you love, look to the glimpse of hope. It is true that they could die from this, but the only thing you can do is wait. They need to make their own decisions, and maybe clarity will come to them in time. Anyone can change. Anyone can be sober. It just takes self motivation.

One last thought: The addict in your life is probably a loved one, a child, a parent, a friend. You love this person. You care about them and their life. It hurts you when they steal from you, lie to you, manipulate you. Please understand that the person you love is under the control of a force so demonic that the true person is suppressed almost to the point of not being there anymore. I guarantee you that this person loves you too, that they would never hurt you in a million years. Separating the addict from the addiction is crucial in dealing with the addict. Remember that when they lash out in anger and start yelling and cursing at you that it is their addiction (demon) doing it not them. The addiction will do anything to protect itself. Love the person who is trapped by this demon, because they are in a living hell everyday and they desperately need you and your love.

Do Not Go Yet; One Last Thing To Do

If you enjoyed this book or found it useful, I'd be very grateful if you'd post a short review on Amazon. Your support really does make a difference, and I read all the reviews personally so I can get your feedback and make this book even better.

Thanks again for your support!

Bibliography:

Ratey, John J., Dr., and Eric Hagerman. "Addiction."
Spark, Little, Brown and
    Company, 2008, pp. 167-90.

"Drug Abuse, Dopamine, and the Brain's Reward
System." *Butler Center for*
    Research, www.hazeldenbettyford.org/education/
bcr/addiction-research/
    drug-abuse-brain-ru-915. Accessed 1 Sept. 2015.

"Helping an Adult Family Member or Friend with a
Drug or Alcohol Addiction."
    Partnership for Drug-Free Kids, drugfree.org/
parent-blog/
    want-help-adult-family-member-friend-drug-
alcohol-problem-7-suggestions/.

Linden, David J. "The Neuroscience of Pleasure." *Huff
Post*, www.huffpost.com/

entry/compass-pleasure_b_890342. Accessed 6
Sept. 2011.

MacBride, Katie. "This 38-year-old study is still
spreading bad ideas about
    addiction." *Pop Science*, theoutline.com/post/2205/
    this-38-year-old-study-is-still-spreading-bad-ideas-
about-addiction?zd=2&zi=nsbqd
    s3q.

"Principles of Drug Addiction Treatment: A Research-
Based Guide (Third
    Edition)." *National Institute on Drug Abuse*,
www.drugabuse.gov/publications/
    principles-drug-addiction-treatment-research-
based-guide-third-edition/
    frequently-asked-questions/why-do-drug-addicted-
persons-keep-using.

"Psychology of Drug Addiction & Substance Abuse
Disorder, Causes & Solutions."
    PsycheTruth, uploaded by Colin Ross, Dr,
www.youtube.com/
    watch?v=8NaHepAgoSg.

"What Does 'Rat Park' Teach Us About Addiction?" *Psychiatric Times*, 10 June

2019, www.psychiatrictimes.com/substance-use-disorder/

what-does-rat-park-teach-us-about-addiction.